V

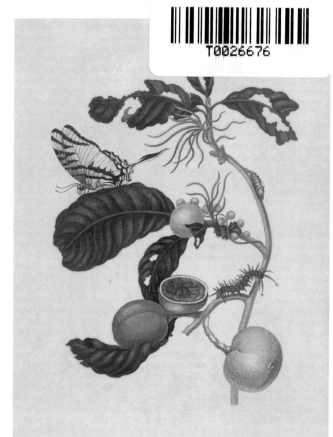

LXXIII

XXIII

As a young girl growing up in the 1650s, Maria Merian was curious about everything. Her hometown of Frankfurt, Germany, was full of creatures that crawled, flew, and scuttled. Butterflies were her favorite insect because their wings held a rainbow of colors.

She could watch for hours as the butterflies flitted around the flowers blooming near her home.

And day after day inside her home, Maria watched her stepfather, Jacob, do something that looked to her like *magic*.

With just a few brushstrokes, he captured blooming flowers and ripe apples on his canvas.

Jacob liked studying plants because they stayed still, and he painted them exactly as they looked.

Maria longed to make her own magic.

Jacob gave her everything she needed in order to paint: tools, lessons, and, best of all, he gave her encouragement.

Unlike her stepfather, after only a few months, Maria grew tired of painting objects that stayed still. She wanted to paint things that crawled, flew, and scuttled—things that *moved*.

She was still curious about all the colorful creatures outside her window—from beetles to moths to spiders—just waiting for her to copy their likenesses on canvas. Maria wanted to study insects and paint them just as they looked, even if she would have to keep her work a secret.

If her neighbors and friends caught her studying bugs, everyone in town would be scared of her.

Unlike Maria, most people in her time didn't want to look at or learn about insects because of superstitions. They believed creatures such as butterflies, moths, and frogs were born from mud puddles in a process known as "spontaneous generation."

These people also believed insects were evil shape-shifters—like werewolves!—and that anyone interested in such creatures was surely evil too. If caught studying bugs, Maria could be considered a witch, put on trial, and punished.

Still, she was determined to understand why such colorful creatures upset grown-ups so much. But there was little printed information on natural history—the history of living things—especially when it came to insects.

Maria hoped to fix that someday.

She started by studying silkworms because they were one of the easiest creatures to find.

When she was sure no one was looking, Maria gently caught the worms and some of their eggs, hid them inside her errand basket, and brought them home, where she could watch and draw them every day.

Maria often touched the silkworms, taking notes on how they then twisted, curled up, or played dead.

She was learning so much just by watching them and their eggs—but she still didn't know what they liked to eat. She worried the silkworms were hungry.

Pretending to fill jugs with water as curious neighbors waved hello, Maria lingered in the silkworms' favorite hiding places to see how they acted in their natural habitat. By noting which plants the worms crawled on most, and gathering some of those leaves for her worms to try, she soon learned their favorite snack— mulberry leaves.

They chose mulberry leaves over everything else Maria offered. Her first experiment with the silkworms—discovering what they ate—was a success!

After that, Maria often found herself inventing errands to run so she could gather supplies for her silkworm studies. She tirelessly collected, observed, and sketched until, one day, something amazing happened—the silkworm eggs hatched! Maria fed the tiny larvae that emerged with their favorite snack.

And all the while, she painted.

Because she had trained as a flower painter, Maria included the silkworms' favorite blossoms and plants in her art.

She wanted to share what she had learned about the silkworms with the townspeople so they wouldn't be afraid anymore.

The more Maria learned and painted, the more questions she had about how the silkworms grew and changed.

When the newly hatched larvae grew bigger, they looked just like mature silkworms. And when the worms produced silk threads to form cocoons, Maria prodded and squeezed them, trying to understand what was happening. She called the cocoons "date pits" because they felt hard like the center of a date or peach.

She knew something was happening inside the cocoon, something she couldn't see.

Maria had to be patient, so she painted while she waited for a change she could observe.

One afternoon, small creatures finally broke free of Maria's cocoons.

Only, they weren't silkworms anymore.

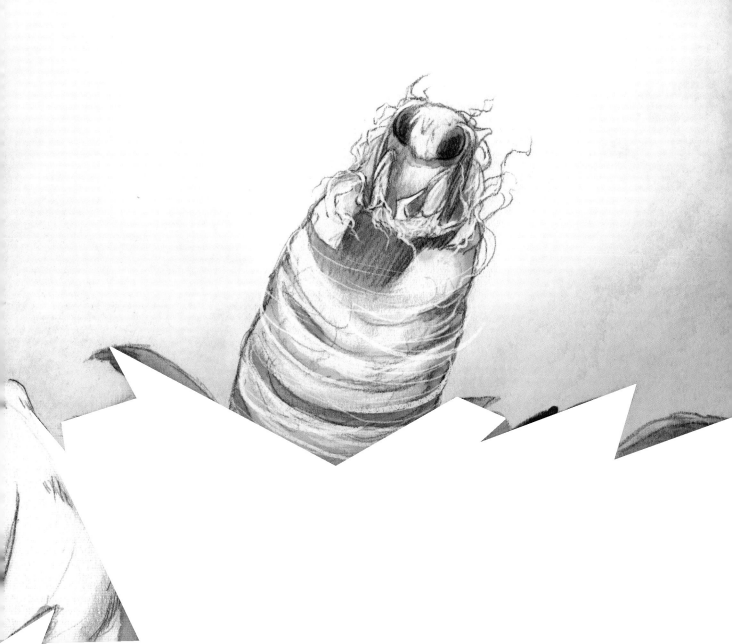

They were beautiful moths with
paper-white wings and frilly antennae!

Maria learned two things that day. First, that there was no such thing as "spontaneous generation." And, second, that grown-ups were sometimes wrong.

Excited to learn more, Maria crept through her neighbors' backyards, smiling and waving whenever anyone looked her way. The moment she was alone, she collected every new type of caterpillar she spotted.

She painted hairy ones, slimy ones, and speedy ones, always
curious to see how they changed and what they ate. She watched
them transform into beautiful butterflies and moths.

Their "shape-shifting" was part of nature, not magic after all.

It was better because the insects did it on their own, through
the process of *metamorphosis*.

Maria still longed to share all she had learned about caterpillars and their amazing transformations with the townspeople. But because of her young age, and because she was a woman, she felt no one in town would believe her.

Secretly, Maria often wondered about what types of insects and other creatures she might find outside of Frankfurt. She'd have to wait until she was married and could leave home. Then she and her husband moved to Nuremberg, Germany, where at just twenty-three years old, Maria taught other girls how to observe, draw, and paint just like she did. She gave her students the tools they needed to study whatever interested them—along with a healthy dose of her curiosity.

And when Maria had a family of her own,
she shared her curiosity with her daughters too.

When she wasn't giving lessons—and sometimes when she was—Maria continued to collect and paint small animals that crawled, flew, and scuttled. She even began to paint ones that slithered and swam. From big, hairy spiders to lizards to tadpoles, there were so many creatures to study that Maria was able to publish a whole book of her art. And then another.

At long last, she was sharing
what she knew with the world.
But she wasn't done
discovering new animals yet.

Maria's passion for insects eventually took her even farther from home—all the way to Suriname, a small country in South America. She traveled to Suriname by boat, on a scientific journey—one of the first of its kind! Maria had heard about colorful lizards, bigger spiders, and different winged insects there, and she was curious about all of them.

Luckily, she had an assistant to help her collect and study these fascinating creatures—her twenty-one-year-old daughter, Dorothea.

In South America, Maria faced new challenges. There weren't any maps to guide her on her insect-collecting expeditions into the rain forest, and the climate was hot and wet, slowing her attempts to search for new insects. The heat made her tire more easily, and the rain made bugs harder to find because they sought shelter from downpours.

Still, her passion for learning kept her exploring through dense rain forests and along the banks of rushing rivers, where she discovered amazing creatures to observe and paint.

After two years of exploring, Maria became
ill and returned home. Yet not even sickness
could keep Maria from her studies for long.
She'd learned so much in Suriname that she
now had enough paintings to fill a third
book. As one of the first female scientists
to study insects, she still wanted to
share her findings with others.
And she kept collecting and
observing bugs wherever
she went…

because Maria never lost her curiosity and fascination for creatures that crawled, flew, and scuttled, a curiosity that had been sparked years earlier when she watched a silkworm transform into a beautiful moth.

Author's Note

Maria Sibylla Merian (April 2, 1647–January 13, 1717) was born in Germany into a family of artists and printers just fourteen years after Galileo Galilei was put on house arrest for his theory that the earth orbited the sun. It was also a time when women weren't honored for their accomplishments and contributions; a time when women artists weren't allowed to paint with oils like men were, having to use watercolors instead.

When Maria was just three years old, she showed such strong artistic talent that her father predicted she would one day become a great painter. After Maria's father's death, Maria's mother married Jacob Marrel, a floral and still life painter who encouraged Maria's talent with a paintbrush. But artistic skill wasn't the only special thing about Maria. Her curiosity and fascination with insects from a young age was unheard of at that time—not many people back then would have dared to pick up an insect, much less bring one home to study it, while the belief in spontaneous generation was so common.

Maria's silkworm studies at age thirteen went a long way toward disproving spontaneous generation, but there weren't many who would listen to a woman, let alone a child, about matters of science at that time. Maria conducted her studies and her insect paintings in secret for fear of being called a witch by her community, something that could have gotten her shunned, hurt, or worse. Of course, Maria knew she wasn't a witch. Maria was a girl scientist, ahead of her time.

After further artistic study and an unhappy marriage, she eventually traveled to Suriname, South America, with her daughter Dorothea. There, Maria continued to paint insects, as well as birds, reptiles, and the plants that nourished each creature in its natural habitat; she even discovered new species of animals and plants. Although Maria achieved her dream of seeing her paintings in books—twice—before her time in Suriname, she was still excited to publish a book about the creatures she encountered there. After that, she started to gain more recognition, with collectors of her artwork ranging from fellow scientists to Russia's czar, Peter the Great. Her paintings helped people to understand the process of metamorphosis, and the relationships between certain plants and small animals. Because of this, she is often credited with being one of the first entomologists.

Thanks to Maria's determination to follow her passion despite what others thought, humanity's understanding of the interaction between insects, animals, and the environment grew significantly during her time. And even though she lived a long time ago, her artwork still inspires and reminds people of how beautiful and interesting insects and reptiles really are.